Praise for *Pages of White Sky*

"In 'A David Hockney Landscape Poem,' when Tim Sherry says, 'It is about the same, same thing—an effort to find a place to find meaning,' he could as well be describing the rest of the poems in *Pages of White Sky*. Many of them are set in specific locations—the Chihuly Garden and Glass Collections Cafe, the Ephesus archaeological site, a farm truck hauling grain in in North Dakota, The Crescent City Lighthouse, a little britches rodeo in Halfway, Oregon—but the real terrain of this collection is always the landscape of the human spirit. These poems are windows left open to it, letting its meaning in."

> —Joe Green, founder of The Peasandcues Press and author of *What Water Does at a Time Like This*

"Approaching like ponies fresh from summer fields, Tim Sherry's poems, skittish and a little wild, transcend their domestication. His forte is deft renditions of the singular daily moments that make up a life. In a poem like 'I Am Not a Gary Soto,' he redeems his admission of a strict religious upbringing by reminding us that the poetic moment is not necessarily dramatic, that sometimes the subtle implications of a father's 'gray flannel suit' is enough. Though they have fed on star shine and moon-brushed grasses, these works have been bred to carry us fast and far, and do so with grace."

> —Chris Dahl, author of *Mrs. Dahl in the Season of Cub Scouts*

PAGES OF WHITE SKY

PAGES OF WHITE SKY

Poems

Tim Sherry

MoonPath Press

Poetry
ISBN 978-1-936657-52-0

Cover photo by Thomas Holt of the painting
"Skagit You Beauty" by Lynn Zimmerman,
30" x 48" oil on canvas, used with permission of the artist

Author photo by Thomas Holt

Book design by Tonya Namura, using Gentium Basic (text)
and Millesime (display)

MoonPath Press is dedicated to publishing the
finest poets living in the U.S. Pacific Northwest.

MoonPath Press
PO Box 445
Tillamook, OR 97141

MoonPathPress@gmail.com

http://MoonPathPress.com

To Marcia, my wildest dream

Acknowledgments

Grateful acknowledgment is made to the editors of the following publications where these poems first appeared, some in slightly different forms:

Cirque: A Literary Journal for the North Pacific Rim, "At Pompeys Pillar" and "Daughter Driving Home to Mother"

For Love of Orcas; an anthology published by Wandering Aengus Press, "My River"

Ice Cream Poems: reflections on life with ice cream, an anthology published by World Enough Writers, "Ice Cream at Church Camp"

Interdisciplinary Humanities, "In a Gallery Filled with Borges Block Prints" and "The Light"

Phrasings in Word and Dance, an anthology published by the Chuckanut Sandstone Review, "The Mountains and Their Road"

Spitball: The Literary Baseball Magazine, "Pick-Up Games"

Thanks to The Puget Sound Poetry Connection of Tacoma, the Olympia Poetry Network, The Deep Water Poets of Steilacoom, and the Striped Water Poets of Auburn where a number of these poems were first read.

Table of Contents

III

PAGES OF WHITE SKY

[When] your days are numbered, use them to throw open the window of the soul to the sun.
—Marcus Aurelius
The Emperor's Handbook

Plinking

A pellet gun is perfect for any day on the trail
shooting at a hanging branch or the glint
of a bottle out of the corner of my eye.
As far off the beaten path as I am most days
in my wilderness, there is no one around
in danger of my aim; but I am careful to look
before pulling the trigger. So too my poetry.

I

If people reach perfection they vanish, you know.
—T.H. White
The Once and Future King

Walt Whitman as Guide

Turning a corner of lilacs, I keep on
towards home
with Whitman on my mind—
and arrive just as family is arriving
for Thanksgiving dinner.
The conversation there
of politics and money and who believes what
is why I went walking—to be ready to be quiet.
In the evening after everyone has left,
I sit near a window
open on the vacant lot across the street
with *Leaves of Grass* on my lap—
reading his sprawls across the page wondering
how it must have been to walk as he did
tramping past carpenters hammering,
millers milling, mothers with their children,
young men robust in their boldness
filling America with their singing
when it was vacant with so much of a future.

No X

Walking for the exercise my doctor recommends,
I am now and then struck by
what comes to mind out of nowhere.
A tree down in the wind or a sagging fence line

starts me thinking after just a glance left or right.
It is then my walking isn't what the doctor ordered,
but what long ago a therapist talked me through—
that life sometimes goes on long walks

with no destination. Oh, for a map at such times,
like the one given to me by the kid next door
when he swore an X marked the spot where treasure
was buried. But no. What comes to mind

is how a fallen tree or an old fence are me. I am
a wanderer in all the stories about wandering.
I am as lost as all the souls ever lost. I am Adam
dead east, Oedipus with my eyes gouged out.

Yes, that is how far I walk sometimes.
There is no road diverged in a wood to explain it.
There is no as the crow flies to get me back
to any understanding of such thoughts.

There is no math or science or theology
or philosophy I have ever known to help me
replant such a tree or repair such a fence.
All I can do is keep walking until I get back home.

Big Trees and Denial

Ten big evergreen trees range your yard.
Ten. You've counted them off
too many times to friends come for the day.
You've carried them like stories from college
to conversations over coffee where
their number jumps around like roosters
in a barnyard trying to get their point across.
You've used them in more metaphors
than means anything anymore.

That is how it must seem as you walk the beach
on the Big Island trying to save the marriage.
In the middle of the Pacific, what is the point
of telling stories from back home where home
is you in an apartment and her in the house?
Comparing trees to anniversaries
can't have much metaphor left beyond the walking,
the talking, the sideways glances to see if anything
might lead somewhere beyond ten years.

When denial is, *It was just one night*, then,
She didn't mean anything, and, *It happened
over a year ago and I haven't seen her since*,
any number is just a number,
any tree just a tree. No meaning. No reason
to listen. Just talk. Her look that finally is
straight into your eyes is what Jesus
must have meant when the cock crowed
and he turned and looked upon Peter.

The Last Fires

Like the last fires of summer that burn
in the mountains, the fall maples blazed red
and orange across the ski runs and clear cuts.

The traffic slowed facing into the sun
on the wide turn at the ten-mile marker
down from the summit behind me,

and a young woman in the next lane over
smiled as I leaned forward to see
where the leaves matched the sunset.

Then she waved and sped away—
leaving me to remember those times
when I wore gold chains and drove fast cars.

Rodeo Dream

Let me sit on the arch
of a rodeo bull's back.
Give me that chance
to reach up and touch
the clouds of my dreams—

to be the cowboy
I played up to eighth grade.
Remove my coat and tie
and put me in boots
and stirrups riding danger.

Keep my one hand
hanging on for dear life
and the other waving as if
conducting a symphony
of *oohs* and *aahs*

from the crowd there
to watch me thrown off.
As I pick myself up
and grab my Stetson,
keep your eye on the bull

circling back for more,
thinking it's not over—
until the clown taunts him
back to the chute where
he disappeared in high school.

Basketball Fantasy

after "96 Vandam" by Gerald Stern

I'm going into the basement where I keep stuff
I haven't thought about for years.
There I am going to dig out the basketball
that taught me the game in the driveway,
the one worn smooth with the 10,000 hours
that were supposed to get me to the NBA.
I'm going to put that basketball in the trunk
of the '52 Buick I found in a New Jersey junkyard
and restored for just this kind of madness.
Then I'm going to drive out into the countryside
where there might still be a boy bouncing a ball
and shooting at a hoop on the side of a barn.
If I should ever find that boy,
I will take the ball out of the trunk
and hope he will let me shoot with him
until the sun goes down and the stars come out.

Downhill on a Skateboard

Cold stars watch us chum...
  —Kenneth Patchen in "Street Corner College"

A Big Wheel on the sidewalk, a Razor scooter
to grade school, junior high on a banana seat Sting Ray
pretending a Harley with high-rise handle bars,
twelve hours a day after tenth grade hanging out
on a skateboard, and it's all downhill from here.

We don't have books in our backpacks. Today
is yesterday again. Who says we need breakfast?

Kicked out is fine with us. Good weed
is our 4 point 0. Don't make us need a summer job.

Rain or shine, the same jeans and hoody.
We won't graduate until we're in jail or dead.

Our role models are the dads who left
and spend their days on barstools. The downhill
of war and guns and hate and cops at our door
is who we have been since we were born,
and the wheels of history is who we are.

Daughter Driving Home to Mother

Out in the desert, Hanford no longer waited.
The tanks, buried in the hurry of The War, had leaked
the secret kept from the wives while the husbands
flirted the science into full romance;
and now the dashboard radio
spoke of water reckless underground.

She couldn't imagine the depth
or what test would tell the harm.
But she knew about contamination—unspoken
in conversation with her mother at the stove,
when fathers kept secrets
and mothers, knowing them, kept the house anyway.

A 3x5 box was her mother's place to keep quiet,
and all the town had known not to ask for her recipes
after the blue ribbons for her pies and preserves
at the fair—though none could have guessed
she sometimes got it wrong with her peaches
and secretly dumped them out on the compost.

The map helped with the big bend of the Columbia
through Richland when nothing else
in the winter landscape gave place to the day.
The smell on the wind was December,
and she had to get to Idaho where mother
needed daughter after father was the talk of the town.

Yesterday, their shouting match of fifty years
ended in police and a reporter at the door
in Lewiston where they had retired.
Now rumors of his secrets,
waiting to surface in tomorrow's *Tribune*,
demanded that contamination be spoken.

Stopped for gas outside Pasco,
she thought she smelled someone's cooking
and remembered her parents' words
from all those nights down the hall—
their red eyes in the morning bent over
breakfast that smelled of weak coffee and despair.

Crossing the Snake, she prayed the words
shouted at *her* last night in Seattle
would stay buried—and not leech into the conversation
while she helped her mother
through the next days and weeks of meals
from recipes she herself had learned by heart.

cap

i know it is not
wise to dream about
what a three-year-old will
become when he is grown but i
just had to buy my big boy a base
ball cap with a yankee logo and the coolest little bill

Cell Phones Still Ringing in Blacksburg

The cell phones in the pockets
of the dead students were still ringing...
       —a news report

a quick sweep of the team into the room
looking for the hand with the gun

careful steps over arms and legs
towards the young man wearing anger and hate

slow lift of the desks clearing the way
to the place he had found for himself in a corner

radios with the trained vocabulary of disaster
unanswered until who is who is who

cell phones still ringing
in pockets in book bags in a clutched hand

all through the morning mothers and fathers
waiting to hear just a *hello*

Breezy Point After Hurricane Sandy

You didn't die. Everything is gone to ashes
and standing water, but you didn't die.
Coming back the day after to just stare,
to join a neighbor who stares too,
is as much house and life as you have left.
The news says more than a hundred died,
names places where they lived,
and shows a photo of a house still there
with a tree down across a car left
by a woman who ran with all she could carry.
You got out with nothing; but you are alive,
standing where your house was.
The neighbor touches your arm and speaks
the words always used for such times and places.
Another neighbor arrives and joins
the two of you. A slight breeze comes up.

Vietnam Vets in Morongo Valley

The trenches were tunnels
where we went down after gooks.
The uniform of the day
was sweat and mud.
Marijuana and beer was our diet.
We waited every day
for the shelling and firefights.
R and R made no sense on any beach.

Home again was turns away
in the old neighborhoods.
There wasn't a single parade.
No one joined the VFW.
There was no such thing
as shell shock—PTSD
was four decades away.
I wasn't back, but I went on
for awhile. Then I couldn't.

This valley was here all along
until I found it on another long drive
to anywhere but home.
The leather jacket on the Harley
I met gassing up—was me;
and I've been here ever since
with the rest of us who went
to Vietnam and never came back.

Small Town Wedding

He had asked again and again about their childhood
promises. But like a little girl behind a curtain
cued with a push and a whisper, anxious
for fear's quiet voice to echo down to nothing,
she had waited in the days after high school
to hear something that could answer.
She had wanted just a little more time to wander
up the hill behind the barns, to sit
beside the headstones that marked the promises
brought across the prairie by her great greats—
and recall the stories told to her all through childhood
to send her on her way. She had let the wait
turn to weeks hoping to hear, each night in bed,
up there above the ceiling of her dreams,
conversations by women that echoed so far out
into the unknown that they never made the news
or the history books. She waited the months
until fall to hear from the cousin in the city
to invite her to come and live and work
her way through college; but the only mail
was letters to her brother about basketball.
She kept on at the Dairy Freeze on the interstate,
tempted between stories of the highway or ice cream
at the end of each day. Seasons turned to seasons
until the valediction of her dreams spoken
the year before at graduation echoed down
to whispers in the new pick-up that he brought back
from the city—and she married that farmer boy.

Dreams on the Wall

Every garage and man cave needs a pin-up
when a man needs a place to go
to work out the details of a wife in the kitchen,
off to the store, at a meeting at church,
always too busy for a Saturday noon vacation.

The rules don't allow any more than
a beautiful girl on the wall or the back of a door
looking at you the way it happens in dreams.
The one your dad had in his garage
wore a swim suit. The neighbor has his
behind the basement stairs wearing nothing at all.
You've heard the pastor keeps a small painting
of an angel with a Marilyn Monroe face
inside his vestment closet. You need
a dream on the wall when the days move along,
and last night she had a headache.

When a buddy notices you have a centerfold
looking at you over her shoulder,
your silence admits what pin-ups are for—
when you have a wife who binges on Netflix
and hardly looks at you anymore.

Dreamballers

With a baseball tethered to a pole, twirled up
and then slowly down to the strike zone,
a boy stood hitting home runs in his driveway.

Next door, a mommy watched a daddy
lob underhand touchdowns to their little boy
bobblehead in his new helmet.

Across the street a dog chewed
at a soccer ball left after the winning goal
just before supper called the girl in.

Around the corner, a teenager in his first tuxedo,
who had rehearsed the moment a thousand times
while shooting free throws in his back yard,
opened the car door for the girl of his dreams.

Veterans Day

Beside the brass doorknob,
gently taped to the etched glass,
a yellow ribbon decal
with *Support Our Troops*
was reminder how upscale coffee shops
need homeless men sitting outside.
And as I carried my latte
to where my car was parked,
there he was around the corner
with his dirty beard and Calvary eyes.
The *Jesus Christ!* cursed by a blue suit
nearly tripping over him
was met with a thousand-yard stare
and a cardboard sign that said
war had done it to him—
and hoped God would do good things
for anyone with spare change
to drop into the empty fried chicken bucket
there where his legs would have been
if he owned a blue suit and a coffee card.
When I stopped with a dollar
and a *Thank you for your service*,
his barely audible *God bless you*
was sad reminder that what I offered
was a drop in the bucket
compared to what is owed
when the streets are full of homeless men
who were there when we needed them.

Tacoma Detention Center

In an industrial park in a town in a state
in our country there is a place to put people
no one knows what to do with because
such people can't get the proper papers
or they wear something on their heads
that isn't a baseball cap. It is a place
more or less for profit in a partnership
between our country and a corporation
that knows what to do with such people.
Let's never call it a jail or a prison.
Let's pretend it is like a room after school
at a junior high where the teachers think
they know what to do about scuffling
or spit wads or talking back or copying.
If we tame it with a word like *detention*
that we use on children and hide it
in a gray building next to a grey building,
it doesn't need to be a jail or a prison
to be a jail or a prison in your town.

Alzheimer Waltz

Music more than memory moved him
among the tables being cleared
after lunch and rearranged
for afternoon bingo. As the staff worked,
the radio playing echoed back
to a 1940s ballroom and an orchestra
ten minutes to midnight.
The limp of the last twenty years picked up
as he approached the window
where a young woman worked at her desk
reviewing the dinner menu.
His tap on the glass, bow at the waist,
and reach of his suddenly steady hand
startled her into a *Yes* nodded up
from her chair and giggled
around the corner onto the dance floor—
where nothing he remembered
and nothing she knew of the waltz
mattered for the next fifteen minutes.

no punctuation

joel meyerowitz and the rest made all those
photographs in the 70s and 80s with no people
in them no one on the porches rocking
in the evening light no one walking the beaches
silhouetted for some kind of romance to soften
the world nothing on city streets except litter
and broken doors and maybe the back of a leg
just turned around a corner always the books
they made for coffee tables had the one picture
on the cover that led you to think they must have
liked edward hopper who made the same kinds
of pictures but with paint and people mostly
just standing there or staring out towards places
that can never be painted places like empty rooms
or long streets they might have wanted to be another
ansel adams who took photographs of big places
that didn't have people either but didnt need them
off there in the distance of the big west
but by the time they got their first cameras
when vietnam was all the picture the new guys
making photographs probably had seen
too many people dead in life magazines or
too many actors standing still doing nothing
but smoking cigarettes in french movies so they
just left people out annie leibovitz has tried to put
them back in but now digital doesnt need people
just their body parts photo shopped from cyberspace
and artificial intelligence will soon convince us
that any photographs of porches or beaches or city
streets dont need real people to punctuate the scene

Bringing It In in North Dakota

His grain is still family farmed on big acres,
and better that way. Bringing it in
on the county road, across the highway into town,
where the school, the church, the grain elevator
are the good life, he knows why it is better—
with people here still starting every day
with a big sit-down breakfast,
and Friday night football a hundred miles away
and back at midnight to meet the team.

His big truck crawls under its load.
The stop at the incline up to the scales
could be a pose for the filmmaker shooting
from under a tree with a rusty tractor
in the foreground. But there is big business
in this small town without even a tavern
or grocery store to keep people out after supper.
There is money in those fields out there;
and in the driver's seat, wearing the oldest hat
in America, he knows it—bringing the load in.

Anywhere else, he could be homeless
looking like he does in a blue shirt faded
to the color of winter sky and jeans
that don't need washing when harvest is on.
There is no rest on days of fifteen hours in the cab
when sunrise and sunset aren't far enough apart.
Even talk at the pop machine takes too much time—
more time than has passed since family farms
brought it in with horse and wagon.

A Little Food Rant

I don't want to read another warning
or ingredients label. I tear out and burn
any magazine or newspaper article
about nutrition. If my doctor starts talking
about cutting down on sweets,
I drift off into reverie about cake.
When it's Thanksgiving and overeating
is the guilt trip, I load up on thirds.
Don't sit there in your size three
and compare how thin I was
in my wedding picture and now
me trying to hide fifty pounds
in stretch jeans and a sweatshirt.
Organic is what you want me to eat?
A thousand fewer calories?
OK. I will ask the neighbor
for some carrots and peas
from his pesticide-free garden,
cut them up as if in a religious ceremony,
mix them into a bowl of ramen,
wash them down with a hand-crafted beer,
and let the push and pull
of the universe have its way.

Made in Washington

In the museum store, the assurance
is also brag that the shelves are pure.
The woman behind the desk makes certain
that you understand why Washington
is better than China or India,
that genuine is not going to fade
in bright sunlight or come apart
where the corners are glued.
You start with dried salmon
and work your way to the rack
of postcards. It is still Washington
when you get to the key chains
where you lose the bet with yourself
they must be from overseas. The wood boxes
and Almond Roca, too, are labeled
with familiar names just up the road.
You want some contaminant
to shake you head at. But at the counter
when you pay for the tee-shirt
with *Tacoma* stenciled across the front,
you finally give up. Then behind you
as you are going out the door,
you hear a little boy asking his mother,
Where is the Yakama nation?

Night Runner

The runner watches up ahead
for the lights of any cars.
The clouds break, and behind the rain
the sky opens across the stars.

Enough day waits back against the trees
to reveal cattle grazing and a dog
walking slowly home. The runner
drops down into a vale of fog—

a dip in the narrow road
where the coming cold of the night
has found a place to wait
until the ending of the light.

The dog keeps on across the field.
The runner slows as he nears
a dim-lit crossroad.
There he turns and disappears.

II

The road must eventually lead to the whole world.
—Jack Kerouac
On the Road

My River

It flows quietly past our small towns
like most rivers civilized long ago,
my river, the Puyallup. Hard to pronounce,
leveed to tame it, fished only by treaty
or license, it is where I follow when I need
a river to take me back to a place remote
where I might know what was lost when
its name was first spoken from a map.

It is not mighty. It is not of any fame.
It works no wonders of flood or heartache.
No literature or song tells of romance
along its banks. It is found on no global map.
To speak of it anywhere east of its mountain
requires humility when so few know of it.

But it is my Mississippi, my Congo, the Nile,
the Yangtze, the Amazon—any great river
one might name. Yes, levees. Yes, bridges.
Yes, fences along its banks. A diversion dam
and a flume using its water for electricity.
Changes of course man-made into Tacoma.

And up past the power plant at Electron,
into the foothills, finally in the deep woods
of the national park, I stand hoping to hear
in the sound of untamed water over boulders
and tree roots what the Puyallups
and Nisquallys and Nooksacks heard along
their rivers coming out of their mountains
down to the saltwater of the Puget Sound.

Elegy for the Five Dollar Fill-Up

At the edge of half-a-town outside Mojave,
a gas pump with the numbers stuck on 25 9/10
is faded from red and green to desert.
Blowing sand and hundred-plus temperatures
take fifty years sometimes; but Main Street
always ends up colorless a mile off the interstate.

The big Cadillacs and Imperials
with their eight-miles-to-the-gallon under the hood
are gone—the way mule teams
coming out of Death Valley
couldn't compete with locomotion
to keep borax rolling to market.

On Memorial Day, at a car show
in downtown Bakersfield, we know *horsepower*
was the wrong word for eight cylinders
when a '59 El Dorado with original paint
has won the judges trophy—
and we wish somehow history had never ended.

Five Amish Girls at the Crescent City Lighthouse

The tide coming in brings five Amish girls
in their strict dresses
down from an afternoon exploring at the lighthouse
to step their way back to reality
across the rocks and wet sand,
eyes down from years of obedience
now finding shells and seaweed of quiet delight.
For what do they come,
so far away from their Pennsylvania—
here where the sea follows no scripture,
requires nothing of man or woman
to keep its rules of coming in and going out?
The rest of us in our swimsuits and beach clothes
can't help but wonder if this is their only frolic—
if their little white caps are beacon
to signal the danger
in what the rest of us are doing watching them.

At the Halfway Little Britches Rodeo

Eastern Oregon holds onto the past
in its small towns
the way out of the way places in the West
so often treat change—
with another beer and a joke
that is philosophy. Highway 86
has passed by the town named Halfway—
a name that must have been a joke
halfway between Pine and Cornucopia
when a trading post grew
to a saloon and a church and a post office
and finally a town with a few years of boom
in its economy. Today
the little britches rodeo hangs on
to the old days of roping and riding,
and we watch from the wooden grandstand
where once was the high school's football field.
Wearing a plastic helmet
instead of a cowboy hat, a six year old
wrangles history on the back of a sheep.
When the sheep dumps him,
tears are part of the lesson
that leftover towns in the West
teach halfway between baby bottles and beer—
and the town folk
nod their heads and chuckle
as the sorriest looking clown
ever seen at a rodeo
helps the little cowboy back to his daddy
waiting at the fence to brush him off
and wipe away the old tears in his eyes.

Docent at the Eisenhower Presidential Library

When you are there to sell hyperbole as history,
sitting at a counter ten steps inside the door
you need a good book or the internet
for the hours it takes. Tuesdays are your longest
days, but your job is to tell the man and wife
from Des Moines that Eisenhower's
Longest Day is still important. They are polite
with their questions about the campus,
as it is called, where his first house, the library,
a museum, his statue are spread like stories
that once were told of good and bad,
right and wrong—stories as simple
as the one word answer, *Ike*, that the husband
heard from his father to explain
what turned the tide that day on Omaha Beach.
You too are polite, trained in the national interest
to point to the campus map, to hand a brochure
to the wife, to walk with the two of them to the door
and gesture across the seven acres
to be sure they visit the Meditation Center
where the tombs are. The husband tells you
they are on a trip to visit all the presidential libraries
in the country, and you stand and watch
as they start out across the park-like setting
it takes for history to keep repeating itself.

At the Tacoma Buffalo Soldiers Museum

The term "buffalo soldier" is said to have
originated in the 1860s when Indian warriors
thought the hair of African American cavalry
looked like the manes of buffalo.
    —various sources

It is not a national place where big names come
when black history is on the calendar.
This museum is in a small town south of a big city
the way the buffalo soldier barracks were down the hill
at West Point. It is marked by a hand-painted sign
at a corner and an American flag hung out
on open days. It could be anyone's house
on any street with a number hard to remember
unless you write it down and put it aside for a day
in the future when you promise yourself you will visit.
There are no more buffalo soldiers; but William Jones,
one of the last ones, made his house, this house,
into a museum and put his life as a soldier on the walls
and in display cases to tell the story of men
who deserved it told. It is where he left behind
a place to tour the out-of-towners around that corner,
down that street, through the front door,
and back to a hundred years of pride
in men doing their duty to their country in spite of hair
that often kept soldiers such as he from living
on certain streets in small towns and big cities.

Redwoods Don't Fall Down

Conversation in the corner at cocktails
stops, and no one is willing to say
what everyone knows
when, *We heard that some redwoods
fell down in a storm*, is just too small.

Such said is not enough
for something a thousand years of size
suddenly horizontal in the tangle
of a notch valley in northern California.

A redwood is no two-by-four
slipped from its prop against a garage
when a little boy rushes past
with a bump in his laughter
and a daddy waiting in the car.

Small words to tell the death of trees
named after generals and gods leave them
just more windfall, with no imagination
to widen an eye or shift a foot.

Redwoods don't fall down in storms
any more than volcanoes send smoke up or
lots of snow falls in a blizzard or
rocks come loose in an avalanche or
cocktails taste good on Friday evenings.

Honeymoon in Death Valley

It is late afternoon and ghost towns
from a hundred years ago wait.
Brochures from the visitor center
tell of Panamint City, Skiddoo.

We can't know how short years of passion
so often ended in emptiness.
But reading of the gold and silver never found,
the borax muled out, excites the conversation.

The old towns are miles away
as her finger follows the end of the day
off the park map, and we decide tomorrow.
A motor home, on its way into the night,
pushes past and rocks the car.

Wildflowers and dust devils wave us
on through the heat of regret until we pull off
to watch a bouquet of light spread colors
of hope and romance across the valley walls.

In the lingering light
behind Telescope Peak and then gone,
her smile whispers love—
and we hope for a hundred years.

In a Gallery Filled with Borges Block Prints

Cordel pamphlets of mid-twentieth century Brazil
contained the folk tales, myths, and local history
of the back country. Woodcuts were printed
on the covers to attract buyers as the pamphlets
hung in the marketplace. Jose Borges is credited
with enlarging the woodcuts and developing them
into the art form that they are today.
—from the gallery brochure

Block prints from the northeast of Brazil
can't be very big unless you make them dance
out from the past where the forest
and the Amazon conspire against anything of size,

unless you fill them with more celebration
than Carnival snaking through each village
stopping to dance the darkness as deep
into the back country as any dancer would dare to go,

unless your fill them with such color the darkness
retreats so far into the white sky that the myths
and the magic of northeast Brazil dance
smaller than any woodcut would ever need to be.

At Pompeys Pillar

The natives have engraved on the face of this rock
the figures of animals &c. near which I marked
my name and the day of the month & year
Friday 25th July 1806
    —William Clark in his journal

Roman legions never marched in Montana, so the sign
for Pompeys Pillar hesitates my foot just east
of the fork of 90 and 94 where the Yellowstone
swings north to find the Missouri.
Too soon after Billings for anyone to need on the map,
too lost in the small print of towns named
after people long dead, such a place with such a name
cannot exist unless posted. A second sign taps the brake
for a look at the map, and there it is—in italics
to mark a national place. Some instinct of discovery
pulls the wheel onto the exit to follow more signs
to a dirt road that takes me back into the middle of history
beside the river, to the remarkable rock
200 feet high and 400 paces in secumphrance
where William Clark must have understood
that word of mouth was not enough for such a place.

I park and read from a tour book—and soon pass
from tourist to time traveler, trying to imagine
the buffalo and Indians that stopped to graze and camp
because of that huge rock there. Any place
along such a river as the Yellowstone would have done.
But the rock drew them back year after year.
It was a place that must have had a name;
but it was instinct that brought them just as surely
as instinct takes me from the car to the visitor center
where volunteers wait the likes of me
with practiced words of greeting and guardianship,

politely patient with all they know about the rock
all the way back to the stories of spirits said to have
rolled it there from the bluffs across the river.

The words of the volunteer leading me to the rock
and up the wooden ramps and paths
built to control instinct are clear that it was a place
to leave something behind. And what was left
were the names carved—Indians first, then fur trappers,
and soon soldiers with survey crews to mark the way
for railroad men following the river with their tracks
laid down as the land was fenced and farmed
away from Indians and buffalo and the gods.
On the face of the gritty rock are the names of those
who came on their journey to find
what was out there beyond the maps,
names carved in hopes that someone such as I
would stop and know that Al Parker and C.E. Werst
and John Ready and F. Supola were here.
But the name that makes it a national place is
     Wm Clark
     July 25 1806
graffitied near *the figures of animals &c.* Indians
had left to confirm that some things are set in stone.

Ending his afternoon at the rock, Clark named it
after Sacagawea's little boy Pompy, then got back
on the river to meet Lewis and travel on—back
to tell Jefferson that no passage to the East was there,
but the Louisiana he had purchased was treed
and rivered and full of game like no heaven could be;
that no passage to the East was there—but the West,
the West. What should one such as I make of this place?
What does it mean that William Clark
gave this rock a toddler's name and signed his own?
He wrote that from the rock he could see

on the northerly side high romantic clifts approach
& jut over the water. I too can feel the romance
of what he must have known—that Pompeys Pillar
was the place to make "and Clark" more
than any journal or word of mouth could tell;
for he brought back no prize or treasure, left no roads
or marble ruins, wrote no epic poem.
William Clark signed his name on the land
that would make America another Rome.

Charlotte's Blueberry Park

You drive along a road that is barely alive,
run down to sofas exploding in yards and porches
full of old Webers and folding chairs. You slow down
to make sure this is still your town.
A man walking wears the look of such neighborhoods.
Then, out of the corner of your eye, you see
off to the left rows and rows of blueberry bushes—
and a sign. Out of the car, you walk to the sign
that is reverent, as if God is still watching here,
in its telling of Charlotte Valbert who wanted
the old farm to stay blueberries and talked the city
into a park where volunteers come during the year
to tend the berries—free to anyone who is willing
to pick them. After you read what sounds like
a miracle in the middle of such a forgotten place,
you follow the path that winds its way to the wetlands
where farming didn't work. It is reminder
that a park needs rough edges the same as a town
needs some of its history sagging on old porches.
The weeds will never be pulled this far from the paths
and mown rows of blueberries. No volunteer
will attempt anything but a warning sign. You turn off
the path where the ground is too much bog
and pick your way to a clearing where you find
what looks like the foundation for a building—a barn
maybe. You stop and look out through the trees
wondering what the houses across the street
from Charlotte's Blueberry Park think of such a place
in a neighborhood such as theirs in a town such as yours.

Road Trip

It was a mom and dad and two brothers on Sunday
drives when gas was a buck. It was a big car—
a Buick, then a DeSoto, and dreams of a Cadillac.
Now it's just you and anything that gets
at least thirty miles to the gallon on a long stretch
for more hours than a hundred Sundays.
Why isn't even a question. It's the DNA
of growing up in the West where driving fifty miles
for a good milkshake was what you did.

Today it's the interstate cutting through farmland
so that you see the back sides of places.
Old is what's left—rusty tractors, sagging clothes lines,
the side of a barn advertising faded beer—until
you see a girl doing what looks like dancing
out of the corner of your eye. She wears a blue dress,
a dress in a place where dresses left for the city
decades ago. You see her spin, and then
seventy-five leaves her where she has to stay.

You are in love with that blue dress, and you want
to turn around and go back, wait fifty years, and
marry that girl. But at seventy-five, it's not Sunday.
One of your brothers is dead. The other one
doesn't drive any more. You are on your way
to visit a buddy from college. You could have flown,
but road trips like this one are few and far between
now—and this may be your last chance
to drive anywhere where there is a girl still dancing.

The Mountains and Their Road

On Google Earth, the road outlines
the Chuckanut Mountains as if a three year old
had gouged a line of black crayon to finish
furious, green coloring.
                         The blacktop hangs
high above the rails built along the water,
all twist and turn where roadbed
was blasted and dug out of the sandstone cliffs.

Along the way, houses pretend ownership
where any flat gives foundation.
                             But falling rock
is reminder every year that the mountains
are still the mountains, that the old way
between Bellingham and Bow is the slow way.

Whoever built such a road must have been drunk
on the same daydreams and dumb luck
as the hang gliders who jump
into the wind from the old logging road
that goes to the top of Blanchard Mountain
and gives a place to view sunsets
when darkness and the mountains conspire.

The young men who dare speed
on Chuckanut Drive depend on the same darkness
for courage when they round the hairpin
at Oyster Creek still at twenty-five and live to tell
of a hundred on the straightaway
past the old farms. But their bragging
tells no reality; for who owns the road?

The conservancy members making signs
to save Blanchard Mountain

from more clear cutting know whose road—
know that with the trees and moss gone,
the rain washing down to fissure, no shadow
on the road, no color to the peaks, the mountains
will send themselves across the pavement,
over the tracks, down to the water.

The sun will set the same at sea level as straight up.
New logging roads will confuse the satellites.
The mountains and their road will no longer
be a place to fly high enough or drive fast enough
for daydreams
              or dumb luck
                       or courage
to matter.

I Wanted a Storm

I wanted our love to be a storm starting
far out on the prairie just down from the Rockies
with the kind of wind at its back
that tears roofs off, the way wild love making
sends sheets and blankets to the floor.

I wanted it to be the kind of storm
that people put a hushed date to
and use as the measure of any storm to come,
the way love after the worst fight
is too dangerous to talk about again above a whisper.

I wanted it to stop at a farm somewhere
in Kansas and pound rain and hail down so hard
that it took days to recover,
the way it has taken years to understand
why such a storm and our love are not the same.

Such love passed us by, off in the distance,
and was followed by the most beautiful summers ever
on the prairie—full of honest work and Saturdays
in town the way true love is full of promises kept
through calmer storms that come and go.

The Light

At Giverny, the buses park,
and the day's travelers line up
to walk the paths in Monet's garden.
They point and remark the colors
in the morning light, but are anxious
to stand in pairs for pictures
of themselves, like models
hired for the day. From guidebooks
they quote descriptions and history
and compare what they see in the sunlight
to what was told the day before
in carefully lighted museums.
Hurried along the paths to the ponds
across the road, they take turns
politely standing on the little bridges
waving instructions
to those with their cameras across the water
where Monet himself might have sat
off in the trees under his big hat.
When a flag goes up on a stick
and the guide calls out directions
to the gift shop and the time
to meet back at the buses,
the ladies clutch their purses
and the men put the cameras away.
They move quickly along, one or two
glancing back with exaggerated last looks,
never to understand why Monet
painted the ponds—why he so often
sat alone and painted the ponds.

Time Zone Meditation

in memory of Tom Hansen

The map is folded open to Burns Junction
in the middle of nowhere, and time
doesn't matter on the highway to New Princeton.
For the next fifty miles in eastern Oregon
there is nothing that needs a name,
and if an open road goes anywhere,
it surely goes to the heart of why the small *T*s
on the map zig and zag down from the Snake
and then back to the state line in Idaho
where no one noticed or cared when the railroads
needed time zones to run on schedule.
You stop at the summit of Duck Pond Ridge
and park where you imagine the line is
between Pacific Time and Mountain Time—
the same as you straddled what to choose
between a clinical trial or another operation
that might give you one year at the most.
When you decided neither, you knew a road trip
under open skies to places with no names
was better treatment than chemotherapy,
or any hope surgery would buy you more time.

Fish Story

for Mark

How many times can the same story be told
without filleting it down to no smell,
no bones to pick out? This time
he told it with photographs for proof,
so it was of a size for belief.
But it was still a fish story, which made it
this big—and we chuckled at the twinkle.

Strangers might not buy the story of a plane ride
in a four-seater, a guide's old pick-up, and then
a mile hike in to the river of dreams
running through such stories. But best of all
when it is said and done are the friends
there to chuckle at the size of such stories,
the way that laughter is hook, line, and sinker.

Cenotaph

If you like to walk through cemeteries
and read the names and dates,
if your eyes turn from the car in front of you
on the interstate to look off to a hill
with a barn sagging back to buffalo,
then take a road atlas with you
and head east on I-90. Decide either
northeastern Montana or head south
from Billings to anyplace in Wyoming.
Find a station on the dial
that plays country western
and preaches Jesus as an American.
Choose someplace where an exit
looks like it has no purpose.
Turn off and follow the two lanes
toward the number four font on the map
that reads like the 1870s
when place names were poetry.
Keep on even though the mile number
on the map halfway there
seems like more miles than the longest trip
you ever took with Mom and Dad
when city living was measured in blocks
and as kids in the back seat you were never there
fast enough even when you got there.
Stop beside the road when you see up ahead
what looks like a town settled
into the curve of the road down to a place
where the map shows there is a river.
Get out of the car and let the wind
put voices in your head that whisper
places you read about in the Hugo collection
you used to write your masters thesis.
Don't wait for another car to pass by

as signal to get back in and drive on.
Stand there as long as it takes to imagine
that town up ahead looking like
every town in every movie you ever saw
about moving west. Remember
what you felt like when the family stopped
at the Little Big Horn in the 1950s
and were told that there was nothing there
to mark the grave of even one Indian.

What to Call It

*Noah didn't name his sculptures because
he wanted viewers to give them their
own interpretation.*
  —Pat Bundy, docent at the museum

When art doesn't need a name, make it personal
and give it a lifetime. Get an old truck and drive
around to junkyards and garage sales
and stop beside the road for lost hubcaps
and gnarled tree limbs down. Take it all
to your ten acres of desert where no one will care
if art is lit by the sun and moon
instead of soft light. Spread one man's treasure
out on tables and on the ground the better to see
what is there. It was junk to the world,
but you know better; so let the wind tell you
how to assemble the story of your life
from old serving trays, dead shoes, bowling balls,
bicycle wheels, TRS-80s, doorknobs, stove pipes,
Tic Tacs, mannequins, Levi's—the archaeology
of a life dedicated to the world
where you found it. When art doesn't need a name,
set it out across the desert and let visitors guess.
At the Noah Purifoy Outdoor Museum
of Assemblage Sculpture in Joshua Tree,
the weeks and months and years of wind
and dust and heat do their part
to change what has no name into what to call it.

Anecdote of a White Chair

because of Wallace Stevens

Someone placed a white chair
back against a row of pines and firs
where a long, open field
makes an acre seem a mile.

The fences along and at the back
of the empty field put a frame
to what might have been a joke,
or someone's idea of art or Zen.

But from the road, one glance
is enough to know a field with a chair
made more white by being there
is not a place for such expanse.

The Poet Seeks His Muse

after "North" by Seamus Heaney

At the end of the road is a place marked
by no mistaken mapmaking,
and Point No Point is indeed its name—
and metaphor for why I am here

on another one-tank trip to another place
on my empty bucket list of ideas,
another place for a Facebook selfie,
another place to seek my muse.

No great battles were fought,
no conqueror plundered, no rush for riches
suddenly happened
as the world found the Northwest.

The Puget Sound gives no inspiration,
whispers no first lines, reveals no great truth
to one man alone on a beach
known, not for its history, but for its birds.

The only epiphany is what is brought,
daydreamed on the ferry to Kingston
and on to here to wait for sunset.
The gulls and loons tell of safe harbor,

here where the lighthouse
needs darkness for its purpose, and where
the cargo ships on their way to Seattle
need the lighthouse on their way.

Sometimes one needs no place such as here
for nothing to happen—
and memory to incubate words
to tell something seen or read or heard;

and in the unmarked darkness, I hear
what I came for—a splash, and then
silence—as if a cormorant telling me,
"Dive instead of drive.

Sit the calm waters of your hindsight,
but then go deep when any stir
beneath the surface invites long foray
into what brought you here.

Compose in darkness with no point,
and find what no one finds
when the Puget Sound offers
no thundering Atlantic, no roaring Pacific."

An Autumn Poem Without Leaves

Write an autumn poem without any of
the things usually included in autumn poems.
—a writing prompt at a poetry workshop

It is the last day of October, and I am
more interested in what the wind is doing
with plastic bags and hamburger wrappers
than what the responsible rake
propped against the garage is for.

I know what wind does to trees in October.
What I don't know is why a woman's bra
would be dangling on a chain link fence
or how a sun-bleached map of Michigan
might have turned up blown
against the foundation of a restaurant in Oregon.

For most people, March is the month
that gets credit for its wind; but give me October
when the wind is the muse who
walks with me.
        I am no Sisyphus with a rake.
I am Odysseus seeking my place in a world
of far away places called by the songs of wild women.

III

Our souls have sight of that immortal sea
Which brought us hither...

       —William Wordsworth
        Intimations of Immortality
        from Recollections of Early
        Childhood

The New York Times as Church

*Washington state is one of the least
churched states in the country.*
        —a news report

The alarm and the beep of the coffee maker
are the church bells to sit you down
to the gospel told by all the saints
who have bylines for their testaments.
In photographs and on television,
you have seen the name above the door
of their cathedral in Manhattan,
so you know what they are telling you comes
from on high—and no effort of faith
is needed for the two hours of all the news
that is made fit for your Sunday morning.
Oh, you are a believer;
but you prefer your day of rest in pajamas
or underwear until noon.
And in the kitchen, the scone is the body,
more coffee is the wine.
From a light breakfast to fruit for lunch,
you need what they tell you need to know
for the coming week. Then, in the afternoon
you will head for the city park
where you will walk the paths until vespers
on your favorite bench with squirrels
and raccoons at your feet—all of which
is as much sabbath as you need to tell everyone
that, yes, you are a believer; but
you don't need church to know there is a god
or something out there that explains
what *The New York Times* is trying to tell you.

Why I Don't Drink

I don't drink because I don't drink,
the same as you might think little girls
shouldn't wear make-up, the neighbor
down the street never goes for take-out.
A good beer is a good beer for most;
and it is jam with toast for some,
honey for others. My brother thought
baseball should always be played
during the day, and who was anyone to say
otherwise? Some like blue when asked
their favorite color. Some love red.
We make our beds one way or another.
My wife sleeps late. I rise at dawn.
And the world turns on and on.

Again, Queen

Put Freddie Mercury with the rest who died too young,
and count me still a fan of the wild that was Queen.
I never was a champion, except when at a ball game
and my team was winning, the pep band was playing,
and I was vicarious. I never rocked anyone
the way Jimi and Janis and The Lizard King could;
but as I listen now again, to my never dreams,
my soul rises. Yes, there is a semicolon in my life,
a before and after, then and now, long hair and bald,
hope and not going to happen. I have outlived
the music I wanted to be. But, let me sit
beside gray groupies at casino concerts. Don't judge me
teary eyed watching public television oldies shows.
Let me stream the Sixties and Seventies
through ear buds into the Eighties
dreaming rhapsody in the bohemia I never dared—
tamed by the desk lamp that is my only spotlight.

A Green Light Coming On

At six a.m., my belief system takes me
out into the hallway down to the kitchen
over to the coffee maker. There
I know that the flip of a switch
and a green light coming on is a fact
of the electrical grid that starts
as a glacier and sends water to a river
that ends up in a reservoir behind a dam.
But I cannot see what happens
inside the turbines at the dam
to make my coffee. Nor can I prove anything
about how my world ended up what it is—
whether it happened with a big bang
or started one morning
with someone we call God deciding
to make it what it is. I'm no scientist,
so the theory of a universe exploding
into existence is too big for me to understand.
And, obviously, I wasn't there to see
if God did what my mother told me he did
to make this world. So to explain.
On one morning of a hundred billion,
billion years of eternity,
my getting up at six a.m. is an act of faith.

Wading Back into the Bible

The shore is long sand and gentle waves rolling in
where flotsam and jetsam washed up
make the beach a place to explore—
the same way coffee shop theologians wander off
to poke their talking sticks at Judges
and Ezra and II Samuel as if to find
the day's answer to why so fascinating, the sea
of stories told of prophets, saints, and kings.
Shoes off, I let a sneaker wave have its way
with my toes touched into Genesis—and then
follow the foam back toward the surf.
Pants rolled, I wade up to my calves
in the stories of Noah and Abraham and Samson
the way Sunday school was safe.
Weaving the line between the tide coming in
and dry sand, it has been years since
I stripped down to my shorts, plunged in,
and swam out to where the stories of Jesus drop off.

Cadenza and the Coriolis Effect

I don't understand opera any more than
I can tell you whether or not it's true
what I heard in fifth grade—that water
goes down the drain clockwise in Lima, Peru
and counter-clockwise in New York City.
It's that way with things
so complicated there have to be big words
or mathematical formulas for them.
But give me a little boy playing with his blocks,
and I can tell you exactly what he means
when he picks up the one he calls a cow
and puts it on a green pillow
that he says is a field of alfalfa. Better still,
walk with the little boy and me
along the fence at the edge of such a field,
the fence that someone thought would help
keep straight whose is whose.
Make it a summer day with billowing clouds
high in the blue sky. Listen with me
as a single whippoorwill is pleased
with the universe. Pick up a stick,
like the one the little boy has in his hand,
and whack at each fence post as we pass along.
Then you will surely know
why I don't need to understand opera
or ever visit New York City or Lima, Peru.

Meditation in the Mirror

I'm not exactly a Zen Buddhist; I'm just old,
which is almost the same thing.
    —Sparrow in *The Sun* magazine

The mirror is both enemy and friend where I understand
the Stockholm Syndrome—in love with my captor,
that old man looking back at me. I never wanted
to be here at this age, looking at myself, the me
locked away in memory but unable to escape back
to all my hair, limber joints, great abs, those old photos.

But it is me there. So what to do but go along,
depend on what is still left, know that there in the mirror
is someone I can still love. He keeps me tied up
in memory. He sometimes tortures me.
When I have doubts about how all this will turn out,
I know I can still depend on him. He's all I have

until I die; and then I wonder if St. Peter or whoever
is the gatekeeper will believe me when I explain
I wasn't treated so badly at the end, that I finished
with quiet years of submission—on long walks
to find still water where I could look down
at my face mirrored as if old age was not my nemesis.

Sacred Places

Sacred places need people
for their history—to walk their paths,
to sit on the benches and eat
their sandwiches. The wind
and squirrels passing through
aren't there to keep Arlington
alive enough to be sacred.
The boys and their fathers
reverent to hear stories of the *Arizona*,
the widows and ancestors
who came back
to place flowers at Gettysburg,
the school children busy
with notebooks following the guides
at Ground Zero,
their quiet talk, smiles and tears,
a hand held for reassurance
are the *forever* whispered of such places.
When no one is there,
below the surface, fish swim past
sunken ships. Before open hours,
a visitor center is a fawn's windbreak.
Street level at midnight is a rat
on its way to another millennium.

Obituary as Still Life

Don't let yours be another drab obituary.
Make it a work of art where the apples in a dish
near a bouquet of roses in soft candlelight
are the best of who you were.
But before you start, ask some questions
about what a still life really is. Can it be something
of you "found" in the garden rows you planted?
You in the background of that family portrait
on the wall, is that you in a still life? All those things
thrown into a kitchen drawer, if taken out
and spread across a counter, are you there
as an old screwdriver? They don't move.
They were put there by you. In the right light
they might look like heartbeat and violin music.
But are they the life you want people to remember?
Or would you prefer something that wasn't you,
but represents you—like the two photographs
you use as bookmarks, the one looking west
at the Rocky Mountains on Highway 14
in Colorado or the one of the tree
where you went off by yourself at age ten
and conquered your fear of heights
and dragons—and your fifth-grade teacher.
The mountains haven't moved. The tree is there
still. But eventually you will be gone;
and in the meantime you have the opportunity
to leave behind who you want people to remember.
So put it down on paper where people can picture
what you want them to see in the light of the candle
burning low next to the bouquet of roses
and dish of apples you have told them was your life.

The Elvis Question

As we chose from our old 45s, we wondered
if anyone will listen to Elvis when Graceland
is just another big, old mansion in Memphis.
On an inside-outside evening in September
with the last days of heat patient,
it was the big question when the beer
was hand-crafted and the chips were from potatoes
grown on organic farms in Oregon. We shouted
the songs as they scratched and skipped
on the old RCA portable from the basement.
One or two could remember all the lyrics,
and the rest of us smiled along, not needing
to know all the words from those days when
four-four time was as far ahead as we thought.

A newlywed couple drifted off
into the back bedroom to explore their vows
just as someone decided we should all go
from house to house on a kind of scavenger hunt
to ask the Elvis question of all the new neighbors
moving in with their children just born
and their music playing from big speakers
each time they cut the grass or washed the car.
We planned it into a contest for the best answer
beyond *yes* or *no* and handed out paper
and pencils to keep track of everything Elvis.
The beer had to go along too
in case anyone slammed a door
and we needed laughter to get to the next house.

Just as we were leaving, the couple came out
of the back room smiling, tucking their shirts
back into their belts. We told them what
we were doing, and they wanted in.

Everyone had a group already, but they went anyway,
just the two of them—not needing any beer
to chaperone their laughter.
                              An hour later,
everyone was back except the couple.
As the rest of us gathered around our answers,
we decided our 45s were no competition
for that music coming out of big speakers,
and the answer to the Elvis question is that nothing
is eternal except good beer and laughter—and
whatever it was keeping those two out in the night.

Smartphone

The girl with the small screen in her hand
tells her hundred and seventeen friends
she is going to the store after she finishes
her homework. Her daddy told her this morning
that their family will be going to Arkansas to visit
grandparents when school is out. The dog
just jumped on her bed and looks so funny
crawling under the blankets.
                                    One of her friends,
not caring about the BFF list, answers
with a catty comment that she is going
to New York City and never has any homework—
and thinks dogs are gross.
                                    A twelve-year-old girl
has never been outside Eden,
but a smartphone where she can have
everything right there in her hand and tell everyone
she knows about everything she knows whenever
she wants is as much temptation as Eve ever knew.

My Own Myth

I want my own myth for my children
to tell their children. I want it to be
about me on the big blue sea
sailing to far off lands, fighting dragons
with my bare hands, finding gold
where fairy tales are told by giant creatures
with human features. I want them
to remember me as not just a father,
but as a man who sang at the Met,
who had a lion as a pet, who once saved
a baby in a storm. The street where I've lived
isn't paved with gold. I drive a sedan.
My job is downtown. But I've dreamed
of renown, of wearing a crown.
My children once thought I was ten feet tall,
so strong I could break boulders.
I wasn't. But as I grow older,
I want my story told big when I die.
I want it to be myth, but not a lie.

Call It God

When you are in a time or place that makes no sense,
or when there are no answers to the big questions
that science can't even answer, call it God.
If a storm comes in a night
that is already the worst of all bad nights of your life,
speak the word softly for balance. When she comes
around the corner with Vermeer light shining
through the window, don't look for angel wings;
just say, *God, you're beautiful.* If you find a flower
pressed in the pages of a mean book,
leave it there for the next person to know
another synonym for God. Don't worry if the word
turns heads and scolds you when church and state
aren't supposed to be together in the same classroom.
When the three-year-old reaches for the heirloom
and it is gone, just like that, in shards on the floor,
explain it to grandma as God at work
remaking the world. Take a walk through a ghetto
where all the big houses were once the place to live
and say hello to God looking back at you
from every empty window and huddled doorway.
Pull up to the gas pump, and watch the numbers
until it could only be God who gives you
the state of Kansas on one tank. Go ahead.
Call it God when there is no explanation,
no accounting for it, no one around with a better word.
Call it God when in a hospital waiting room
you are praying and there is a stir at the door.

Imagine You Are a Chaos Theory Physicist

Imagine you walk around all day
with a black hole in your head, and you have
a favorite chair where you sit to think,
a chair that one might find at a thrift store
as if put there by an old man's daughter
cleaning out the house after he has ended up
in a wheelchair in the hallway of a nursing home.
Imagine sitting there with monster math
talking to you in God's language—
and you understand that the world
didn't happen in a bang, didn't need
only six days, didn't spin off
from a hurtling asteroid and then kept spinning
for a thousand million years
until green pastures and blue skies appeared
to be explained by art and poetry
and the first words of a small boy
playing in the dirt as if he knew the universe
like the back of that hand reaching out
on the ceiling of the Sistine Chapel.
Imagine yourself getting up out of that chair
to take an evening walk with the dog;
and after a hour under the stars,
the math in your head tells you again
what no words can explain. Most of us
have to-do lists or post-it reminders
as the math of our daily lives.
But imagine coming back in
and sitting back down in that chair,
where you understand what old men and women
in nursing homes are telling us when they
speak gibberish and sing nonsense songs.

Ice Cream at Church Camp

There's no ice in the New Testament.
So standing in line after vespers,
waiting the opening of the snack shop,
the question is so church camp
when someone wonders
if Jesus would have served ice cream
for dessert at the Last Supper—
had there been such a thing in his day.
It's more of the silliness
that sometimes seems so gospel
where such questions
are refrigerated most of the year
under ten feet of snow—
and deciding in the heat
of a summer evening
which flavor, cone or dish,
how many scoops, is just as important
as answering, *What would Jesus do?*

Chad's Crossing

It remains the corner where Chad at 16 was killed—
with a friend on the way to some kind of life
so hard to speak because he died before it happened.
What's to say about an unopened knife?

He did nothing wrong. He even wore his shoulder belt.
Afterwards, we asked so many times the Why.
He had turned that way for home a thousand times.
At church we read some poems less traveled by.

But none of what was said made much sense.
No one could explain a big sedan so far
across the center line that Chad ended
dead a hundred feet beyond his little car.

No coffin suited such as that. Quick cremation
was the only way to do a body so torn
from life. We bore his ashes up his favorite trails
at twilight—deep up into the hills to mourn.

Soon, no words came or went. No Old Master
painted him into a scene. A local group of M.A.D.D.
put some flowers and a white cross beside the road.
We dedicated the yearbook to Chad.

A year later, the traffic light failed again.
The years widened to include a left turn lane.
The epitaph now mentioned by just one or two
is that for Chad's marker, a crossroad must do.

The Zeroes

Each zero, a birthday card comes
with some kind of joke about how old.
Pictures flash with hats on and banners
in the background. Careful cakes
with crooked numbers frosted in front
of the zeroes are marched out with more jokes.
Then, after everyone leaves and the wrap
and ribbons are saved,
                              life is again
hours and days and weeks of just that.
The years between the young zeroes
each had their firsts to make them memories—
loose teeth, bikes, a broken arm. Then
high school, that first solo drive, a real job,
the wedding, a house, baby, baby, baby...
and between the zeroes after that
ellipses signifying so much more or less.

Ancestry and Me

I want something exotic to show on my pie chart,
maybe a sliver in blue from Mongolia
or a small percentage of Cheyenne—
something that lets me be more than another
European descended to a small town
in North America. It doesn't have to mean
I give up my white picket fence
and pick-up truck. I cannot but still want
to look acceptable at the golf course
and not be profiled at airports. But at times
when I wonder what I would be if not me,
I imagine myself on a walkabout in the Outback
or at a pool of water in east Africa,
looking down, wondering who is reflected there.

At Ephesus

Marble is enemy as the noon sun
empties water bottles.
The guide with her numbered flag
reassures at least direction,
and we hope she will standstill
her history under the single tree
long enough for salvation.

Most of the once big city
is now a thousand years of dirt
with stone of uncertain shape
dug out and laid out
the way we sort puzzle pieces.
A small hammer and geometry
work on scaffolding nearby.

Fatigue of the day
discourages questions,
and we press on towards
the amphitheater where
twenty-five thousand seats wait.
The guide explains the acoustics
still work to the top.

St. Paul heard the same,
but knew that preaching there
would send scripture up too high,
and Rome would have him stay—
not to speak more about holiness
but to let the sun compete
with baptism. In the distance,

small hammers work on
as we wait for those
who have climbed to the top seats
pretend to be audience for friends
pretending there are apostles on the stage.
The guide's wink knows
what the sun will soon enough do.

The Creation of the World as Flash Fiction

In so many hundred words or less,
you write a story about a beautiful garden
in a land watered by flowing rivers
and filled with creatures great and small.
A man and a woman live happily there,
before ever after, until one day
the woman does what women sometimes do
when they are naive to the ways of the world—
and God is a man she has to obey.
When the man in the garden finds out,
he does what men sometimes do
when women are naive, but beautiful.
Together, they realize what they have done
is wrong, and they face a future of sadness
and travail. But you don't want the reader
to think the story ends there;
so you send the man and the woman
on a journey without telling the reader
how the story will finally turn out. You roll it up
and leave a copy in a hidden place, like a cave,
where it will one day be found and included
in a book of other flash fiction where all kinds
of writers try to put a happy ending to the story.

Sunday Mornings

What is divinity if it can come only in silent
shadows and in dreams?
        —Wallace Stevens in "Sunday Morning"

I

Somewhere in barns and burned out houses
stink mixes with old horse blankets and bedding;
but there too is life waiting another turn.
Who can say what to do when cancer
is patient to pause awhile, and then goes on
with the dying? When the sparrow falls,
God can count again His place in lives and times.
The unraked maple leaves are the same story.
Watch a beached whale struggle its last two days
and know the sea's salvation in slow time.
After the storm, nothing more than drain water
is how it is told. Every night is more
of the same but with bumps and old nightmares.
When all is darkness, a mother and child may,
or may not, be answers to all the questions asked.

II

Dreaded thoughts wait in the back yard
against the fence rotted to forty-five degrees
of someday on someone's to-do list.
The wait for the right time is always worse
than finding answers to the questions
by doing something—anything. Busy betters
sitting there. Rage, rage was one answer.
Anything with feathers might give someone hope.
A song of oneself sung loudly is better than
nicotine and a radio at midnight. Who can make

the darkest rainy 3 a.m. more than another
worst day than you? You. Wear a good coat.
Step out into the coming dawn.
Turn into the wind and journey with those
who have found their answers on Sunday mornings.

Intimations of Immortality in a Cafe

I love to find beauty in everyday objects.
—Dale Chihuly

Looking down at the tabletop that is a shadow box
filled with fish decoys, we wonder at anyone
who would build a restaurant
with the architecture of an attic. Across the aisle,
a man and woman are chuckling
as they count the toy house trailers
parked where their tabletop is window to the soul
of the glass god of Seattle. Who would
ever think that Mexican silver ashtrays
or 1950s alarm clocks would be
part of any immortality? Pocket knives
and inkwells and bottle openers might be answers
to the big questions of life and death;
but why accordions hanging overhead as if
suspended in the belief that heaven is just a ceiling
away? We all have our stashes of this and that,
our drawers and closets full of what mattered when
our worlds were as simple as a toy truck or a Barbie.
And here, at the Chihuly Garden and Glass
Collections Cafe, we too chuckle—and talk
of our collections of how beautiful things used to be.

In Memory of Alan Hedman

December, 2018

There are no engineers
to make life a straight line,
perfect measure,
just as the creature in the woods
zigs and zags—
not to get anywhere,
but to find what is there
along the way.

If exactitude is your religion,
truth forever the same,
you will miss
what is off to the left,
or hidden behind a curtain.
Stop and read between the lines.
Pretend purpose,

but add aimless now and then.
Find the angle of repose
where life slides.
Walk with someone
who wanders down paths
where you may end up lost
on your way
to another day of discovery.

IV

If you have the words, there's always a chance you'll find the way.

—Seamus Heaney
Stepping Stones: Interviews with Seamus Heaney

I Am Not a Gary Soto

I am not a Gary Soto to write of walking
out the door in the morning
knowing that twelve hours of picking grapes
is the migrant version of a paper route.
I do not have skin color that kept me
at the back of the bus like a Langston Hughes.
I can't imagine being Emily Dickinson
in a man's world or Sylvia Plath
living with demons every day.
Choose any name that drank, and I am not
him—even though I have no reason
not to mix alcohol and ink other than
having been raised by Missouri Lutherans.
When it came to war,
I was no William Stafford to object;
so I did the best I could
to just avoid the whole thing.
I have no idea what it must be like
to have been in the closet with the wrong gender,
so to be an Auden or a Ginsberg
is impossible born the way I am.
A victim of abuse? No. No addictions
other than chocolate. Not a Cherokee or Navajo.
Not descended from one of the six million.
Belief that there is a God and OK with it—
up to the point where it's not too literal.
Married with children. Never out of work.
More or less healthy. Enough money.
No, I am not a Gary Soto—
with not very much to write about other than
maybe the gray flannel suit my father wore.

Eating an Orange at My Desk

after reading "Why I Am Not a Painter" by Frank O'Hara

I have never eaten an orange anywhere
other than in the kitchen or on the patio,
so sitting here at my desk eating an orange
is not only a once-in-a-lifetime experience;
it may be an act of individual freedom.
I wonder if a squirt of juice from my peeling
this orange will make a stain
that, like a snowflake, is unlike
any other stain in the history of the world.
If someone were watching me,
he or she might *tsk, tsk* the possibility
of my making a mess of my desk.
But I can't worry about the echo in my head
of my mother teaching me table manners.
How to gather the peelings from my desk
and throw them away—on the compost
or in the waste basket—is a decision
I have never had to make before.
Everything about eating an orange
at my desk raises questions. But right now,
it is nothing other than doing as I please—
maybe because I know there is no word
in English that rhymes with *orange*.

When a Rose Is Not a Rose

In this poem about a bowl of cereal and a bouquet
of flowers nearby, the cereal is Cheerios,
which sounds close enough to call it rhyme.
And the bouquet? It is roses, which one might suppose
is enough to call this poetry—as such a flower
is the kind of thing found in ode or song.
But what do we call it when the roses, wilted
from yesterday, don't look much like a roses,
the Cheerios are eaten, and the bowl is put away?

Mountain Metaphor

You decide to head to The Mountain because
the neighbor came over yesterday and told you
it is the best summer at Rainier since the 70s
when he reached the summit in tennis shoes.
It doesn't matter that you never go anywhere
that requires walking, let alone hiking. It just seems
like a good idea when the wife and kids are away,
the same way Tom Ewell thought it would work
to let Marilyn Monroe scratch his seven year itch
in the movie named the same as what

you have been feeling the last few months.
So you scramble in the basement for some shorts,
dig out the boots you bought for Breakaway,
or whatever it was called when all the frosh
went to the lake to hike and canoe
and team build for five days to warm up for college.
There was some itching going on there too,
but you can't remember her name. Some of what
you don't want to remember was the poison oak
you got into the only time you really needed boots.

Anyway. You paper sack a sandwich and carrots,
grab sunglasses, fill the water bottle,
decide on the Yankees hat, put in sunscreen,
and throw an extra shirt in the back seat—
knowing you forgot something
the same way you feel when the boss calls you
to bring everything you have to his office
because a board member has just dropped in
and wants to see how the work is going
at the job where you are the project manager.

The road up to the park is more slicked up
than you remember from when you were a kid
and your parents took you. Back then it was
logs and dogs. Now it's composite siding and llamas
on Highway 7 through Elbe up to Ashford.
The park entrance is twenty cars deep.
At Longmire the rangers are busy, but a woman
from Germany is more than willing to tell you
about the trails. You slow down to look, but
the Nisqually Glacier no longer comes down to the road.

At Paradise, the parking lot is full. You drive around
and finally settle on an *Unloading Only* spot
to grab a soda inside the visitor center.
The girl ahead of you in line, bragging about her walk
with her service dog all the way to Camp Muir
at ten thousand feet, makes the mountain a metaphor
you don't now want in your movie—any more
than you will want to explain to your neighbor
that you tried to eat your lunch in your car
before a delivery truck honked you back to reality.

Pick-Up Games

You remember the playground where
no one picks you, not even for right field,
because they know you can't hit.
But you hang around
until someone has to go home for supper.
By the time you get your first ups,
the sun is in your eyes
and you don't even make contact.
It's almost dark when
you get your second time at the plate
and you know your only chance
is to square around and lay one down,
hope it stays fair and you can beat it out.

Today you're sitting at a bar
an hour after work on a Friday,
and the girls at the table near the window
pick the guy sitting next to you—
a big guy with perfect hair and a Rolex.
He'll get at least a triple,
probably a home run.
After a few minutes, the sun is low
through the window right at you.
You shade your eyes and think you see
him already rounding first base.
Off to the side, you notice a girl
who seems to be looking your way.

You turn, and hope you can bunt your way on.

What I Know

to Marcia

I am doing what I'm told to do in the workshops
I attend to learn what I don't know
about writing. In those workshops
held in libraries and churches and bookstores,
and sometimes at retreats in the mountains
or near the sea, I am told to write what I know—
that I can't write in someone else's shoes.
So here is what I know. I know the alarm clock
at five a.m. is not my mother any more
with breakfast ready. I know everything
my father taught me about hard work
and doing the best you can even when you can't
is hard work. Some of the things I know
from a bike down long summer roads are secrets
I need to keep secret. I have forgotten
most of what I know from all the books I've read,
but I know that I read them. I'm glad
I know how to do things around the house
now that plumbers and electricians
cost more per hour than we paid for the house.
Knowing a lot of people has ended up
with maybe a couple of good friends—which
I know is typical for men. Yes, I know
this is a sort of list poem, and often
list poems are dismissed at writing workshops
as something to avoid, like love poems.
So, in a nutshell of what I know, the bottom line,
the essence, the most important thing I know
is that I love you, even though I don't know
how best to say it—other than do
what I learn at workshops and write what I know.

I Used To Be My Name

For years I answered to my name.
Known for what I did and
what I had done, it was enough of a name
in the small pond where I've lived
that often I heard it greet me
from across a room or loudly smiled
walking into a wedding reception.
My name had been in the news
for the kinds of things that got me
pats on the back because strangers
had a few good dreams through me
on the playing field, and they think
that after a little glory in college,
I've had a full ride ever since.
More than a few times my name
got me a better job. Once, just my name
was enough for an invitation
to meet and greet someone whose name
everyone in the world knows.
But after my wife went back to work
and our children started making names
for themselves, I stepped aside
and became her husband
at her office parties and their father
in gymnasiums and at recitals.
Now I am the old man who shows up
at daycare to pick up a three year old
whose mother is married to the name
I used to answer to—and I answer
to whatever name the three year old
calls me when we pretend
she is a princess and I am
her coachman driving her to the ball.

To M—

I lay awake one night and finally lost count of the sheep.
So I practiced memory and thought back on the good
times I never dreamed I would ever need again.
An hour, another, one a.m., baseball cards,
my own bedroom, high school games,
dorm philosophers, honeymoon in
Yellowstone, lake-side rental,
through the glass at pink,
our own address, two,
three o'clock and
I was asleep—
dreaming
of just
you.

Upon Reading a Book of Very Short Poems

Can one line be a poem?

Are more white spaces than words
poetry hidden somewhere between the lines?

Is a read-in title really
nothing more than the poet doesn't know
what to call it?

If one word is twenty spaces
off by itself, does that mean it is orphan
to what the rest of the words
are trying to be?

If no caps or punctuation are there,
is it just random thoughts
out a car window at seventy miles and hour?

If the last poem takes two pages,
does it realize what it is doing ?

If the last page is blank, is that a poem?

Shakespeare on Beer

I would give all my fame
for a pot of ale and safety.
        —Shakespeare in *King Henry V*

A coaster with a brewery name
catches the warmth of the evening
dripping from your glass.
A guy from the neighborhood
has stopped too and quotes Shakespeare
to let everyone in the room know
that beer is one of man's oldest
and best friends. Along the bar,
a search engine of shouts
scrolls beer quotes from all over literature.
The bartender clicks on one
and recites the poem it is from.
Sitting near the window,
you look up from your laptop
where you have been trying to finish
work brought home from the office,
and you raise your glass to the best site
to find true meaning in the world.

Driving an Alphabet Car

Below the picture of an apple is the letter Aa,
and the boy seems to make the connection.
I say the letter out loud. He says it.
We say it together and move on
to Bb and a bear on the next page.
It is a book for toddlers—and a new father
like me who knows the alphabet, but not since
Dick and Jane. At Cc, we are in the car
with a barking Ddog. It doesn't matter that Ee
is an elephant trumpeting in the back seat.
A Ffrog croaks, but a Ggiraffe walking
across the road doesn't make a sound.
We stop and get out to watch a Hhorse.
It is standing next to an Iigloo which is
in a Jjar. We turn the page, and a Kkangaroo
is jumping over a Llion. A Mmouse
flies across the sky on a piece of cheese.
The story gets sillier and sillier, and a man
wearing a Nnecktie is sitting on an Oostrich.
Pp and a pelican pops up. Then a Qqueen.
A Rrooster crows. A Sseal barks.
A Tturkey gobbles what looks like
Thanksgiving dinner. It starts to rain
near the end, so an Uumbrella
keeps us dry as we turn the page—
and there is a woman playing a Vviolin.
It gets a little dangerous when we get to Ww.
There is water everywhere, and of course
Xx is a xylophone as we float past.
A Yyak is waiting there on the next-to-last page
as if this were a story about a drive
through a Zzoo in an alphabet car
with giggling and pointing along the way.

Remembering Names

I can't remember people from most of my years
or from the movies I've seen. I never had days
and nights of lovers, and even if I had, their names
would be gone the way I recognize melodies
but have forgotten the lyrics. I don't know
bird names. I can't tell you what tree is there
on the corner. Apples are apples.
There's a *whatchamacallit* under the hood
that keeps batteries from going dead. That one
is the wrench I use to fix the sink.
Who are all the presidents? I've read and heard
them said; but my mind doesn't work the way
some can recite from the Bible or tell you
the capital of Maine. Yes, I do remember
where I was when Armstrong walked on the moon,
and what I was doing when I heard Kennedy
was shot. But the rest is library tables
where I ground out a degree, children needing
mundane rather than magic, jobs only different
in how far the commute. Tragic? Perhaps.
But I know what to call the star in our sky.
Any berry is my favorite pie. I dream the woman's
name sleeping in my bed. I have stopped to smell
the roses along the way; and it doesn't matter
their names. I remember them as always red.

My Wildest Dreams

I wanted to ride a white stallion
across the Pampas
to meet a senorita
with me in her eyes.

I hoped for a twin engine seaplane
to land in Honolulu
when grass skirts
didn't need imagination.

I wished for a ticket
on the Trans-Siberian Railroad
with a seat next to
Svetlana with blue eyes.

I imagined myself
riding into Paris in 1944
in a Jeep covered with flowers
thrown by adoring women.

I fantasized
crewing on a clipper ship
sailing into Tokyo
and into the arms of a Geisha.

But when I walked into that cafe
and saw her sitting there,
ever since my wife has been
the woman of my wildest dreams.

The Physics of Love

Holding a hand
such as hers,
smelling of the lotion
she uses
to make touch
a law of nature,
I am struck
by how often
gravity lets go
and the sound
of her gentle voice
lifts me up, up
to a place
I never dreamed
was there.

The Damage We Require of Ourselves

Right off, I admit I stole the title of this poem
from the back of a book of poetry.
I won't tell you which book; and if you go
looking for it in all the bookstores in all the world,
even one somewhere on a Greek island
run by expats who use romance as a drug,
even if you go through all the attics in Manhattan
and then multiply that by the number of stars
in the sky above Wyoming, even then
you probably won't find the book of poems
that has such words on its back cover.
But you don't need to. The words are there
in the title of this poem; so you can read them
as if they are just as important as being in the Bible
or the Declaration of Independence
or having been said by Confucius. They are true
anywhere you could read them—in your eyes
looking at yourself in the mirror after a hard night
or in the silence after an apology for the wrong
you did that same night. We can't help
but know that we damage ourselves
given the things we do, even the little things
like tell a white lie, eat too much pie,
drink too much and still drive home
on the Fourth of July. You know you do such things.
You know it and you do them because you have to.
We all have to—in order to fit in in a world going mad
with all the desire and hurt and loneliness
and doubt and loss that fill all those books of poetry
in the bookstores and attics around the world.

What It Is, *Ars Poetica*

Here it is, the moment I tell you
what it is I do and call it poetry.
There are times when it goes on,
it just is, it rhymes or doesn't,
it looks like what people expect
but reads like a drunk letter.
But now I tell you straight out
that whatever it might say,
I mean it to be floating on air
like the clouds of misunderstanding
when sudden death occurs
and we want answers. I put it there
on the page and do not care
that it might be folded
into a paper airplane and sailed
back at an English teacher.
Give me a place to read it aloud
and I will not mind if there is
screechy music interrupting it
played by a five-year-old
on a toy saxophone.
And in the end, if you laugh at it
because of what it is,
I will laugh too—and then pull back
the same curtain where wizards hide
what it is they pretend to do.

Haiku Cat

Perhaps the cat lying in the sun
through the April window,
not moving except a twitch of tail
at some ancient instinct,
is waiting to feel a single strand
of DNA from Basho's cat—
to then get up, stretch,
and move to a different room
where a soft breeze ticks, ticks,
ticks a single apple blossom
against a window there. Perhaps not.

Frisbee Life

A dog in the park last week
entertained the picnics
running and jumping poetry
into the air to catch a frisbee
and bring it tail-wagging back
to a man who could send that frisbee
to the moon if you asked him.
And a little boy did,
pointing to a tree
about two Montanas away.
The dog knew what that meant
and hunkered—
waiting for the man
to *one, two, threeee* that frisbee
on its way to outer space.
Rocket launch
doesn't describe that dog in the air
after that frisbee;
and that is how I would like
to have lived my life too.

Regret

I never learned to dance, really dance
the way it happens in movies—
with a beautiful woman when the moon is full
and an orchestra is playing Cole Porter.
I know how to put the left hand up
and put the right hand in the middle
of the back at about the T-8 vertebrae.
I know to lead, but not be a cowboy about it.
But the Fred and Ginger things of how close,
what to do with my two left feet,
when to turn this way or that,
those things that make dancing dancing—
I don't know how to do those things very well.
It's mostly because I never learned how to ask.
I shuffled. I made eye contact sideways.
I grabbed a hand instead of holding it
on the way to the music. Not knowing
how to even ask is like not knowing
how to move out into traffic on the interstate,
and then ending up with horns behind you
for the next two miles too slow in the slow lane.
An elegance of purpose is key to success
just as much as knowing what to do about it.
Which is why dancing with a beautiful woman
in the moonlight is something I will never do.
And if that isn't something to regret, then
moonlight and music and movies are nothing
more than moonlight and music and movies.

The Same Poem

In fact, most poets write the same poem
over and over.
        —Richard Hugo in *The Triggering Town*

My muse is a book-lined room, family pictures
on the wall all the way back to the old country,
grandchildren's toys in the corner, my wife
still asleep in the only bed we've ever owned,
a radio playing the songs that were
what I always wanted to be, a road map spread
open on the table, a window above my desk,
a maple tree in the yard, each October
two squirrels putting in for winter,
in May a woman next door scratching
at her flowers, every morning
the sound of the coffee pot finishing its perk,
and the keyboard—waiting for another poem
about a room, old photographs, superheroes
and trucks, the love of my life, an oldies station,
a map, a window, a tree, two squirrels,
a woman at her flowers, and a cup of hot coffee.

A David Hockney Landscape Poem

After you have read the title of this poem,
you should probably take another look
at what might lead to a landscape poem
of any kind, let alone one that is part
ekphrastic and part the result of too much coffee.

Where to look is the question
since you probably don't have a coffee table book
of Hockney landscapes. You could ask someone
if he or she has such a book. You could go
to the library and try to find one.

Surely no one you know has one of his landscapes
hanging on the wall. So, thank goodness
for the internet where you can find anything.
Go there and you will find under his name
and IMAGES as many of his landscapes as you want.

You need to look at some of those with rolling hills
and winding roads. Maybe a couple
with a lonely road through empty trees.
There will be some with buildings, but very few
with people. Click, click until you get the feel

for what he is trying to do, and you will
eventually understand this poem. You have read it
before. It is about the same, same thing—
an effort to find a place to find meaning.
If it hadn't been a Hockney landscape

it could have been an Edward Hopper cityscape
or a Monet or Turner, even a Georgia O'Keefe
whose flowers close up are landscapes.
Take a look at them too, and you will see
more of what this poem is about.

It has no winding roads or dark corners or lily pads
or misty Londons or flowers as big as New Mexico.
But it is the same landscape—
where I travel through every day
alone in words and lines on pages of white sky.

I write to remember.

—Terry Tempest Williams
Erosion

About the Author

Tim Sherry is a husband and father, a grandfather and great-grandfather. He earned a B.A. in English from Pacific Lutheran University and an M.A. in English from the University of Chicago, after which he was a long-time public high school teacher, coach, and principal. He has lived in Chicago and for a short time in Europe, has traveled widely throughout the United States, but has always called Tacoma, Washington home.

For most of his life he kept his writing private with only a few attempts at publication. But with the support of writers in the Tacoma, Auburn, and Olympia writing communities, since 2002 he has had poems published in *Rattle, Crab Creek Review, The Broad River Review, Cirque,* and *The Raven Chronicles,* among others. He has been a Pushcart nominee, had his work recognized in contests, and his work has appeared in anthologies. His first full-length collection, *One of Seven Billion,* was published by Moonpath Press in 2014, and *Holy Ghost Town* was published in 2019 by Cirque Press.

In his wildest dreams, he never could have imagined...

timsherry@comcast.net

CPSIA information can be obtained
at www.ICGtesting.com
Printed in the USA
FSHW012357191120